ALL THE REASONS I LOVE BEING AN ACCOUNTANT

ALL THE REASONS I LOVE BEING AN ACCOUNTANT

A Comprehensive Look At Why Being A CPA is the Most Exciting and Under Appreciated Career in the World

Jeffrey Lee

With Jeff Slutsky

© Copyright 2013 by Jeff Slutsky

All rights reserved. This book may not be reproduced, in whole or part, in any form or by an means electronic or mechanical, including photocopy, recording or by any information storage and retrieval system now known or hereafter invented, without written permission from the author.

ALL THE REASONS I LOVE BEING AN ACCOUNANT
To order this book on line go to: www.createspace.com/4551849

ISBN-13: 978-1494344856
ISBN-10: 1494344858

Dedication

This book is dedicated to all those hard working accountants out there. You are depreciatated.

ALSO AVAILABLE BY BY JEFFREY LEE

All The Reasons To Love Obamacare
To Order: www.createspace.com/4476479

All The Reasons Michigan Is Better Than Ohio State
To Order: www.createspace.com/4526469

OTHER BOOKS BY JEFF SLUTSKY

More Smart Marketing
Smart Selling
From The Big Screen to the Real World
Totastmaster's Guide To Successful Speaking
How To Get Clients
Street Fighter Marketing Solutions
No B.S. Grassroots Marketing

ALL THE REASONS I LOVE BEING AN ACCOUNTANT

THIS PAGE IS BLANK DUE TO LACK OF REASONS

ALL THE REASONS I LOVE BEING AN ACCOUNTANT

THIS PAGE IS BLANK DUE
TO LACK OF REASONS

ALL THE REASONS I LOVE BEING AN ACCOUNTANT

THIS PAGE IS BLANK DUE TO LACK OF REASONS

ALL THE REASONS I LOVE BEING AN ACCOUNTANT

THIS PAGE IS BLANK DUE TO LACK OF REASONS

ALL THE REASONS I LOVE BEING AN ACCOUNTANT

THIS PAGE IS BLANK DUE TO LACK OF REASONS

ALL THE REASONS I LOVE BEING AN ACCOUNTANT

THIS PAGE IS BLANK DUE TO LACK OF REASONS

ALL THE REASONS I LOVE BEING AN ACCOUNTANT

THIS PAGE IS BLANK DUE TO LACK OF REASONS

ALL THE REASONS I LOVE BEING AN ACCOUNTANT

THIS PAGE IS BLANK DUE TO LACK OF REASONS

ALL THE REASONS I LOVE BEING AN ACCOUNTANT

THIS PAGE IS BLANK DUE TO LACK OF REASONS

ALL THE REASONS I LOVE BEING AN ACCOUNTANT

THIS PAGE IS BLANK DUE TO LACK OF REASONS

ALL THE REASONS I LOVE BEING AN ACCOUNTANT

THIS PAGE IS BLANK DUE TO LACK OF REASONS

ALL THE REASONS I LOVE BEING AN ACCOUNTANT

THIS PAGE IS BLANK DUE TO LACK OF REASONS

ALL THE REASONS I LOVE BEING AN ACCOUNTANT

THIS PAGE IS BLANK DUE TO LACK OF REASONS

ALL THE REASONS I LOVE BEING AN ACCOUNTANT

THIS PAGE IS BLANK DUE TO LACK OF REASONS

ALL THE REASONS I LOVE BEING AN ACCOUNTANT

THIS PAGE IS BLANK DUE TO LACK OF REASONS

ALL THE REASONS I LOVE BEING AN ACCOUNTANT

THIS PAGE IS BLANK DUE TO LACK OF REASONS

ALL THE REASONS I LOVE BEING AN ACCOUNTANT

THIS PAGE IS BLANK DUE
TO LACK OF REASONS

ALL THE REASONS I LOVE BEING AN ACCOUNTANT

THIS PAGE IS BLANK DUE TO LACK OF REASONS

ALL THE REASONS I LOVE BEING AN ACCOUNTANT

THIS PAGE IS BLANK DUE TO LACK OF REASONS

ALL THE REASONS I LOVE BEING AN ACCOUNTANT

THIS PAGE IS BLANK DUE TO LACK OF REASONS

ALL THE REASONS I LOVE BEING AN ACCOUNTANT

THIS PAGE IS BLANK DUE
TO LACK OF REASONS

ALL THE REASONS I LOVE BEING AN ACCOUNTANT

THIS PAGE IS BLANK DUE TO LACK OF REASONS

ALL THE REASONS I LOVE BEING AN ACCOUNTANT

THIS PAGE IS BLANK DUE
TO LACK OF REASONS

ALL THE REASONS I LOVE BEING AN ACCOUNTANT

THIS PAGE IS BLANK DUE TO LACK OF REASONS

ALL THE REASONS I LOVE BEING AN ACCOUNTANT

THIS PAGE IS BLANK DUE TO LACK OF REASONS

ALL THE REASONS I LOVE BEING AN ACCOUNTANT

THIS PAGE IS BLANK DUE TO LACK OF REASONS

ALL THE REASONS I LOVE BEING AN ACCOUNTANT

THIS PAGE IS BLANK DUE TO LACK OF REASONS

ALL THE REASONS I LOVE BEING AN ACCOUNTANT

THIS PAGE IS BLANK DUE TO LACK OF REASONS

ALL THE REASONS I LOVE BEING AN ACCOUNTANT

THIS PAGE IS BLANK DUE TO LACK OF REASONS

ALL THE REASONS I LOVE BEING AN ACCOUNTANT

THIS PAGE IS BLANK DUE TO LACK OF REASONS

ALL THE REASONS I LOVE BEING AN ACCOUNTANT

THIS PAGE IS BLANK DUE TO LACK OF REASONS

ALL THE REASONS I LOVE BEING AN ACCOUNTANT

THIS PAGE IS BLANK DUE TO LACK OF REASONS

THIS PAGE IS BLANK DUE TO LACK OF REASONS

ALL THE REASONS I LOVE BEING AN ACCOUNTANT

THIS PAGE IS BLANK DUE TO LACK OF REASONS

ALL THE REASONS I LOVE BEING AN ACCOUNTANT

THIS PAGE IS BLANK DUE TO LACK OF REASONS

ALL THE REASONS I LOVE BEING AN ACCOUNTANT

THIS PAGE IS BLANK DUE TO LACK OF REASONS

ALL THE REASONS I LOVE BEING AN ACCOUNTANT

THIS PAGE IS BLANK DUE TO LACK OF REASONS

ALL THE REASONS I LOVE BEING AN ACCOUNTANT

THIS PAGE IS BLANK DUE TO LACK OF REASONS

ALL THE REASONS I LOVE BEING AN ACCOUNTANT

THIS PAGE IS BLANK DUE TO LACK OF REASONS

ALL THE REASONS I LOVE BEING AN ACCOUNTANT

THIS PAGE IS BLANK DUE TO LACK OF REASONS

THIS PAGE IS BLANK DUE TO LACK OF REASONS

ALL THE REASONS I LOVE BEING AN ACCOUNTANT

THIS PAGE IS BLANK DUE TO LACK OF REASONS

ALL THE REASONS I LOVE BEING AN ACCOUNTANT

THIS PAGE IS BLANK DUE TO LACK OF REASONS

ALL THE REASONS I LOVE BEING AN ACCOUNTANT

THIS PAGE IS BLANK DUE TO LACK OF REASONS

ALL THE REASONS I LOVE BEING AN ACCOUNTANT

THIS PAGE IS BLANK DUE TO LACK OF REASONS

ALL THE REASONS I LOVE BEING AN ACCOUNTANT

THIS PAGE IS BLANK DUE TO LACK OF REASONS

ALL THE REASONS I LOVE BEING AN ACCOUNTANT

THIS PAGE IS BLANK DUE TO LACK OF REASONS

All The Reasons I Love Being An Accountant

THIS PAGE IS BLANK DUE TO LACK OF REASONS

ALL THE REASONS I LOVE BEING AN ACCOUNTANT

THIS PAGE IS BLANK DUE TO LACK OF REASONS

ALL THE REASONS I LOVE BEING AN ACCOUNTANT

THIS PAGE IS BLANK DUE TO LACK OF REASONS

ALL THE REASONS I LOVE BEING AN ACCOUNTANT

THIS PAGE IS BLANK DUE TO LACK OF REASONS

ALL THE REASONS I LOVE BEING AN ACCOUNTANT

THIS PAGE IS BLANK DUE TO LACK OF REASONS

ALL THE REASONS I LOVE BEING AN ACCOUNTANT

THIS PAGE IS BLANK DUE TO LACK OF REASONS

ALL THE REASONS I LOVE BEING AN ACCOUNTANT

THIS PAGE IS BLANK DUE TO LACK OF REASONS

ALL THE REASONS I LOVE BEING AN ACCOUNTANT

THIS PAGE IS BLANK DUE TO LACK OF REASONS

ALL THE REASONS I LOVE BEING AN ACCOUNTANT

THIS PAGE IS BLANK DUE TO LACK OF REASONS

ALL THE REASONS I LOVE BEING AN ACCOUNTANT

THIS PAGE IS BLANK DUE TO LACK OF REASONS

ALL THE REASONS I LOVE BEING AN ACCOUNTANT

THIS PAGE IS BLANK DUE TO LACK OF REASONS

ALL THE REASONS I LOVE BEING AN ACCOUNTANT

THIS PAGE IS BLANK DUE TO LACK OF REASONS

ALL THE REASONS I LOVE BEING AN ACCOUNTANT

THIS PAGE IS BLANK DUE TO LACK OF REASONS

ALL THE REASONS I LOVE BEING AN ACCOUNTANT

THIS PAGE IS BLANK DUE TO LACK OF REASONS

ALL THE REASONS I LOVE BEING AN ACCOUNTANT

THIS PAGE IS BLANK DUE TO LACK OF REASONS

All The Reasons I Love Being An Accountant

THIS PAGE IS BLANK DUE TO LACK OF REASONS

ALL THE REASONS I LOVE BEING AN ACCOUNTANT

THIS PAGE IS BLANK DUE TO LACK OF REASONS

ALL THE REASONS I LOVE BEING AN ACCOUNTANT

THIS PAGE IS BLANK DUE
TO LACK OF REASONS

All The Reasons I Love Being An Accountant

THIS PAGE IS BLANK DUE TO LACK OF REASONS

ALL THE REASONS I LOVE BEING AN ACCOUNTANT

THIS PAGE IS BLANK DUE TO LACK OF REASONS

ALL THE REASONS I LOVE BEING AN ACCOUNTANT

THIS PAGE IS BLANK DUE TO LACK OF REASONS

ALL THE REASONS I LOVE BEING AN ACCOUNTANT

THIS PAGE IS BLANK DUE TO LACK OF REASONS

ALL THE REASONS I LOVE BEING AN ACCOUNTANT

THIS PAGE IS BLANK DUE TO LACK OF REASONS

All The Reasons I Love Being An Accountant

THIS PAGE IS BLANK DUE TO LACK OF REASONS

ALL THE REASONS I LOVE BEING AN ACCOUNTANT

THIS PAGE IS BLANK DUE TO LACK OF REASONS

ALL THE REASONS I LOVE BEING AN ACCOUNTANT

THIS PAGE IS BLANK DUE TO LACK OF REASONS

ALL THE REASONS I LOVE BEING AN ACCOUNTANT

THIS PAGE IS BLANK DUE TO LACK OF REASONS

ALL THE REASONS I LOVE BEING AN ACCOUNTANT

THIS PAGE IS BLANK DUE TO LACK OF REASONS

ALL THE REASONS I LOVE BEING AN ACCOUNTANT

THIS PAGE IS BLANK DUE TO LACK OF REASONS

ALL THE REASONS I LOVE BEING AN ACCOUNTANT

THIS PAGE IS BLANK DUE TO LACK OF REASONS

ALL THE REASONS I LOVE BEING AN ACCOUNTANT

THIS PAGE IS BLANK DUE TO LACK OF REASONS

ALL THE REASONS I LOVE BEING AN ACCOUNTANT

THIS PAGE IS BLANK DUE TO LACK OF REASONS

ALL THE REASONS I LOVE BEING AN ACCOUNTANT

THIS PAGE IS BLANK DUE TO LACK OF REASONS

ALL THE REASONS I LOVE BEING AN ACCOUNTANT

THIS PAGE IS BLANK DUE TO LACK OF REASONS

ALL THE REASONS I LOVE BEING AN ACCOUNTANT

THIS PAGE IS BLANK DUE TO LACK OF REASONS

ALL THE REASONS I LOVE BEING AN ACCOUNTANT

THIS PAGE IS BLANK DUE TO LACK OF REASONS

ALL THE REASONS I LOVE BEING AN ACCOUNTANT

THIS PAGE IS BLANK DUE TO LACK OF REASONS

ALL THE REASONS I LOVE BEING AN ACCOUNTANT

THIS PAGE IS BLANK DUE
TO LACK OF REASONS

ALL THE REASONS I LOVE BEING AN ACCOUNTANT

THIS PAGE IS BLANK DUE TO LACK OF REASONS

ALL THE REASONS I LOVE BEING AN ACCOUNTANT

THIS PAGE IS BLANK DUE TO LACK OF REASONS

ALL THE REASONS I LOVE BEING AN ACCOUNTANT

THIS PAGE IS BLANK DUE TO LACK OF REASONS

ALL THE REASONS I LOVE BEING AN ACCOUNTANT

THIS PAGE IS BLANK DUE TO LACK OF REASONS

ALL THE REASONS I LOVE BEING AN ACCOUNTANT

THIS PAGE IS BLANK DUE TO LACK OF REASONS

ALL THE REASONS I LOVE BEING AN ACCOUNTANT

THIS PAGE IS BLANK DUE TO LACK OF REASONS

ALL THE REASONS I LOVE BEING AN ACCOUNTANT

THIS PAGE IS BLANK DUE TO LACK OF REASONS

ALL THE REASONS I LOVE BEING AN ACCOUNTANT

THIS PAGE IS BLANK DUE TO LACK OF REASONS

ALL THE REASONS I LOVE BEING AN ACCOUNTANT

THIS PAGE IS BLANK DUE TO LACK OF REASONS

THIS PAGE IS BLANK DUE TO LACK OF REASONS

ALL THE REASONS I LOVE BEING AN ACCOUNTANT

THIS PAGE IS BLANK DUE TO LACK OF REASONS

ALL THE REASONS I LOVE BEING AN ACCOUNTANT

THIS PAGE IS BLANK DUE TO LACK OF REASONS

ALL THE REASONS I LOVE BEING AN ACCOUNTANT

THIS PAGE IS BLANK DUE TO LACK OF REASONS

ALL THE REASONS I LOVE BEING AN ACCOUNTANT

THIS PAGE IS BLANK DUE
TO LACK OF REASONS

ALL THE REASONS I LOVE BEING AN ACCOUNTANT

THIS PAGE IS BLANK DUE TO LACK OF REASONS

ALL THE REASONS I LOVE BEING AN ACCOUNTANT

THIS PAGE IS BLANK DUE TO LACK OF REASONS

ALL THE REASONS I LOVE BEING AN ACCOUNTANT

THIS PAGE IS BLANK DUE TO LACK OF REASONS

ALL THE REASONS I LOVE BEING AN ACCOUNTANT

THIS PAGE IS BLANK DUE TO LACK OF REASONS

ALL THE REASONS I LOVE BEING AN ACCOUNTANT

THIS PAGE IS BLANK DUE TO LACK OF REASONS

ALL THE REASONS I LOVE BEING AN ACCOUNTANT

THIS PAGE IS BLANK DUE TO LACK OF REASONS

ALL THE REASONS I LOVE BEING AN ACCOUNTANT

THIS PAGE IS BLANK DUE TO LACK OF REASONS

ALL THE REASONS I LOVE BEING AN ACCOUNTANT

THIS PAGE IS BLANK DUE TO LACK OF REASONS

ALL THE REASONS I LOVE BEING AN ACCOUNTANT

THIS PAGE IS BLANK DUE TO LACK OF REASONS

ALL THE REASONS I LOVE BEING AN ACCOUNTANT

THIS PAGE IS BLANK DUE TO LACK OF REASONS

All The Reasons I Love Being An Accountant

THIS PAGE IS BLANK DUE TO LACK OF REASONS

THIS PAGE IS BLANK DUE TO LACK OF REASONS

ALL THE REASONS I LOVE BEING AN ACCOUNTANT

THIS PAGE IS BLANK DUE TO LACK OF REASONS

ALL THE REASONS I LOVE BEING AN ACCOUNTANT

THIS PAGE IS BLANK DUE TO LACK OF REASONS

ALL THE REASONS I LOVE BEING AN ACCOUNTANT

THIS PAGE IS BLANK DUE TO LACK OF REASONS

ALL THE REASONS I LOVE BEING AN ACCOUNTANT

THIS PAGE IS BLANK DUE TO LACK OF REASONS

ALL THE REASONS I LOVE BEING AN ACCOUNTANT

THIS PAGE IS BLANK DUE TO LACK OF REASONS

ALL THE REASONS I LOVE BEING AN ACCOUNTANT

THIS PAGE IS BLANK DUE TO LACK OF REASONS

ALL THE REASONS I LOVE BEING AN ACCOUNTANT

THIS PAGE IS BLANK DUE TO LACK OF REASONS

ALL THE REASONS I LOVE BEING AN ACCOUNTANT

THIS PAGE IS BLANK DUE TO LACK OF REASONS

ALL THE REASONS I LOVE BEING AN ACCOUNTANT

THIS PAGE IS BLANK DUE TO LACK OF REASONS

ALL THE REASONS I LOVE BEING AN ACCOUNTANT

THIS PAGE IS BLANK DUE TO LACK OF REASONS

ALL THE REASONS I LOVE BEING AN ACCOUNTANT

THIS PAGE IS BLANK DUE TO LACK OF REASONS

ALL THE REASONS I LOVE BEING AN ACCOUNTANT

THIS PAGE IS BLANK DUE TO LACK OF REASONS

ALL THE REASONS I LOVE BEING AN ACCOUNTANT

THIS PAGE IS BLANK DUE TO LACK OF REASONS

ALL THE REASONS I LOVE BEING AN ACCOUNTANT

THIS PAGE IS BLANK DUE TO LACK OF REASONS

ALL THE REASONS I LOVE BEING AN ACCOUNTANT

THIS PAGE IS BLANK DUE TO LACK OF REASONS

ALL THE REASONS I LOVE BEING AN ACCOUNTANT

THIS PAGE IS BLANK DUE TO LACK OF REASONS

ALL THE REASONS I LOVE BEING AN ACCOUNTANT

THIS PAGE IS BLANK DUE TO LACK OF REASONS

ALL THE REASONS I LOVE BEING AN ACCOUNTANT

THIS PAGE IS BLANK DUE TO LACK OF REASONS

All The Reasons I Love Being An Accountant

THIS PAGE IS BLANK DUE TO LACK OF REASONS

ALL THE REASONS I LOVE BEING AN ACCOUNTANT

THIS PAGE IS BLANK DUE TO LACK OF REASONS

ALL THE REASONS I LOVE BEING AN ACCOUNTANT

THIS PAGE IS BLANK DUE TO LACK OF REASONS

ALL THE REASONS I LOVE BEING AN ACCOUNTANT

THIS PAGE IS BLANK DUE TO LACK OF REASONS

ALL THE REASONS I LOVE BEING AN ACCOUNTANT

THIS PAGE IS BLANK DUE TO LACK OF REASONS

To order more copies of this book on line:

www.createspace.com/4551849

Also Available:

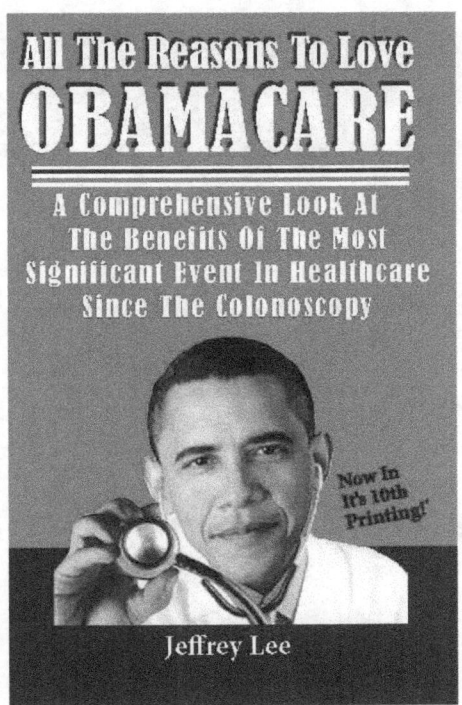

www.createspace.com/4476479

To order *More Smart Marketing:*

www.createspace.com/4403184

To order *Smart Selling:*

www.createspace.com/4411673

www.ingramcontent.com/pod-product-compliance
Lightning Source LLC
Chambersburg PA
CBHW051710170526
45167CB00002B/615